Skyhorse Publishing books may be purchased in bulk
at special discounts for sales promotion, corporate
gifts, fund-raising, or educational purposes. Special
editions can also be created to specifications. For
details, contact the Special Sales Department, Skyhorse
Publishing, 555 Eighth Avenue, Suite 903, New York, NY
10018 or
info@skyhorsepublishing.com.

www.skyhorsepublishing.com

10 9 8 7 6 5 4 3 2 1

Things drunk people say / edited by Kathleen Go.
        p. cm.
   ISBN 978-1-60239-642-5 (alk. paper)
 1. Drinking of alcoholic beverages--Humor. 2.
Alcoholics--Humor. 3. Conduct of life--Humor. I. Go,
Kathleen.
   PN6231.D7T47 2009
   394.1'30207--dc22

2009013958

Printed in China

for the talkers.

introduction

People talk. Or so I've heard. And drunk, talking people I've definitely heard.

I can only remember a few times in my life when I've regretted the things I've said—the moments in anger, in passion, out of spite, carelessly, insensitively. All those other times, I'd been sober. Suffice it to say that my own quotable drunk moments have wisely been repressed. But I have to say it: Talking under the influence is a pretty effective method of communication. Slurring and lisping aside, I'd argue that it helps improve projection and candor. It makes friends and it lightens moods. It shows that you can be in touch with your emotions, albeit briefly and tumultuously. Most important, it's fucking hilarious.

There is little bar-goers
love to hate (or just
plain hate) more than an
intoxicated train wreck,
especially if the train
wreck won't stop talking.

Case in point: One time
I stumbled into a twenty-
minute conversation with
a girl who couldn't stop
crying over how badly her
shoes hurt her feet. In
between her sobs and my
laughter, she went off on
some boisterous tangent
about how I "don't know
how it looks to be her,"
that "people have a lot
more things going on on top
of the surface," and that
"not everyone can handle
the life [she] never got to
have." Yeah, it didn't make
any sense to me either, but
I'm glad I got front row
seats to that freak show
because it kept me laughing
for the rest of the night.

You see? While drunk talk has its ups and downs, sober talk can never beat drunk talk's entertainment value.

Drunk talk lets you finally get that nagging peeve off your chest in a sloshed, overdue scream out; say "I love you" for the first time (sigh, guilty); bask in a surge of bravery and break up with that asshole of a boyfriend or girlfriend; smother someone who doesn't care with your dark family history; make a best friend in someone who agrees the line to the bathroom is totally long; or generally dive into inappropriate, obnoxious, yet fun, random pleasantries. Frankly, sober talk is drunk talk's bitch.

Try huddling up with your
boys to tell them you love
them and wouldn't be the
person you are without
them. Cry on the sidewalk
because everyone left you
alone again for being
your rowdy, dance-on-the-
bar-while-wearing-a-skirt
the-way-you-did-when-you-
were-eighteen self. Tell a
colleague what you really
think about your boss. Tell
your boss. Break it to your
roommate that you're pretty
sure she has multiple
personalities and they're
all psycho. Can you really
do it sober? I'd commend
you if you truly could, but
this isn't that kind of
book.

Drunk talk has no limits—
something you will learn
in the coming pages, and,
if you should be so lucky,
in life. But it does
have stages that range
from mistakenly sober
to unmistakably wasted.
These drunk quotes begin
relatively tame, gradually
get progressively absurd,
and eventually, finish as
delightfully offensive.
The quotes you're about to
encounter were conceived
in the vulnerable brains
of drunk people, overheard
by bystanders, passed on
to me, shoved into a very
pretty box, and re-gifted
to you. You're welcome.

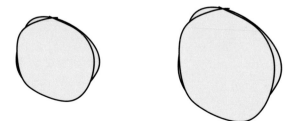

Nothing serious, here. You're only beginning to smile goofily, and because your acquaintances have seen your liquid intake, they're not throwing the "Had a little too much to drink there?" and "Oooh! Someone's drunk" around yet. (Good thing, too. The Getting There stage is the only stage in which trite, pseudo-accusations won't anger you. Moving forward, however, your defensiveness against people who rightly accuse you of being drunk will triple. And that's because there's an enormous stage between tipsy and obliterated in which you become too aware of your intoxication, and begin to border on paranoid. But I'm getting one stage ahead of myself.)

getting
there ...

So you're smiling goofily.
You generally have
control over your basic
motor skills ... but hold
that thought. For some
reason, it's important
that you comment on a
bystander's similar
taste in shoes, to laugh
over it until your
interaction fizzles into
awkward silence because
you're still sober
enough to know neither
of you really gives a
shit. And then for some
reason, you must know
said bystander's alma
mater. And maybe share
your weekly cigarette
with this person. (See:
"I only smoke when
I drink.") For some
alcohol-fueled reason...

Those are salmonella candles.

Oh yeah, I used to put the salmonella spray on all the time.

Jager bomb?

Oh, no thanks, I moved out of my parents' house years ago.

I should have stopped drinking at 2. You should have stopped drinking when you were nineteen.

Waffle Fries from Chick-fil-a are the BEST...

EXcept for the ones with the little coats on them.

she says,

"joely! you were s'posed to say YES.'

and i'm like,

"what? no blowjob for 6 months
and you're s'posed to get a YES?!"

HOW OLD IS?
KELLY RIPA!

I WOULD LOVE TO HAVE
SEX WITH HER.

...SHE LIKE FORTY-THREE?

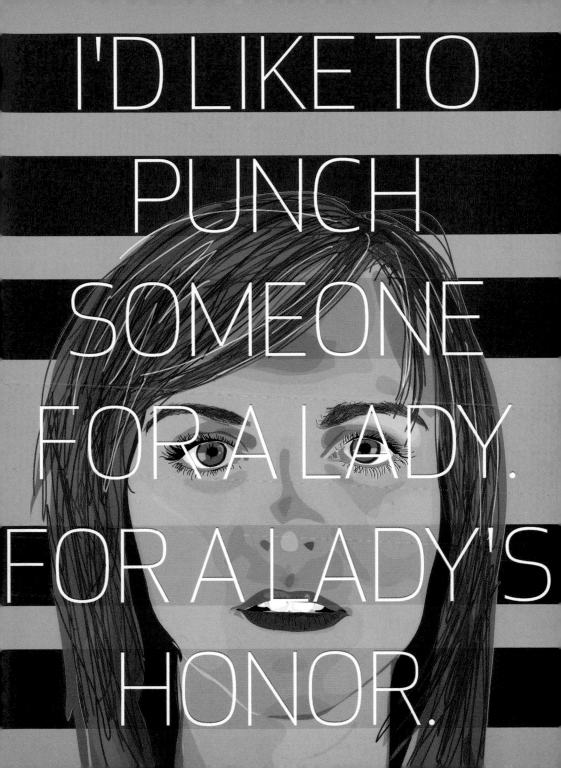

pregnancy is the new hangover.

DON'T HER LIPS GET ALL MUSHY WHEN SHE STARTS TO GET DRUNK?

Yeah, dude. She looks like a Dreamworks character.

YEAH. OR PLAY DOH.

Girls taking shots is not sexy.

It's about as sexy as those shirts they wear that already come with belts.

She'd be cute if
she wasn't so fat.

She would have gone home with him
if he didn't have fetlocks.

Get the duct tape. You have dropped your last beer.

We got REM.
We got Jenga.
It's pretty much Friday night.

Oh hey!
That's the shirt you're wearing in your default!

IT'D BE SWEET TO BREAK A BABY'S HAND.
WHAT DID I TELL YOU MY NAME WAS?

It smells like I just did three lines of that Ramen chicken flavoring.

want me to spit in your mouth?

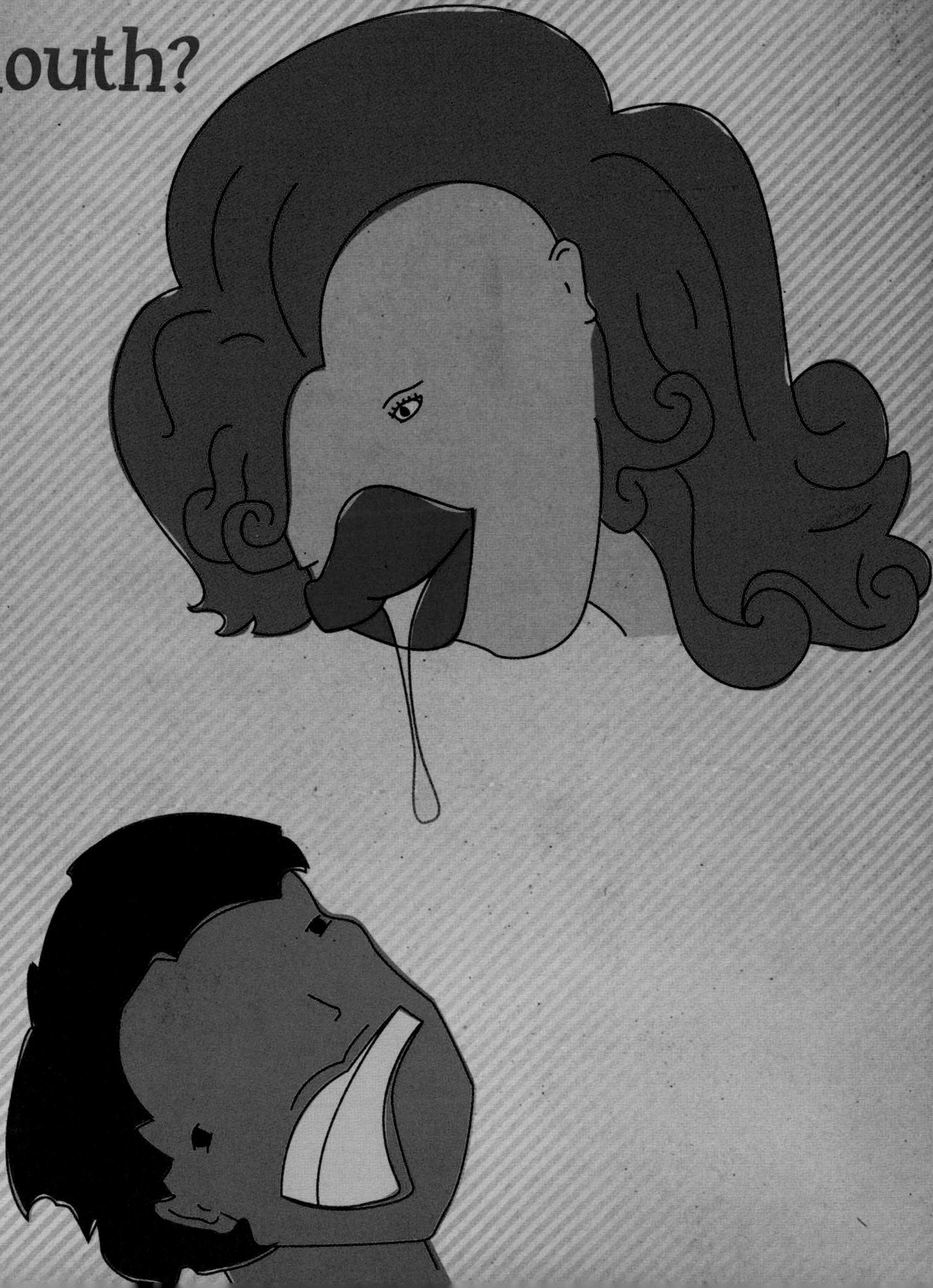

This looks like a promising place for head.

Hey, I left my skirt at your house last night. Can you give it to my brother when you see him?

What's the matter with you?

i thought diaphragms
were from like the 1800s

That's the girl
that was blowing
lines off the toilet
seat last weekend

THAT IS THE GAYEST WATER EVER... **THAT DRINK COULD MARRY A DUDE IN CONNECTICUT.**

Oh! So get this shit:
I'm pregnant.

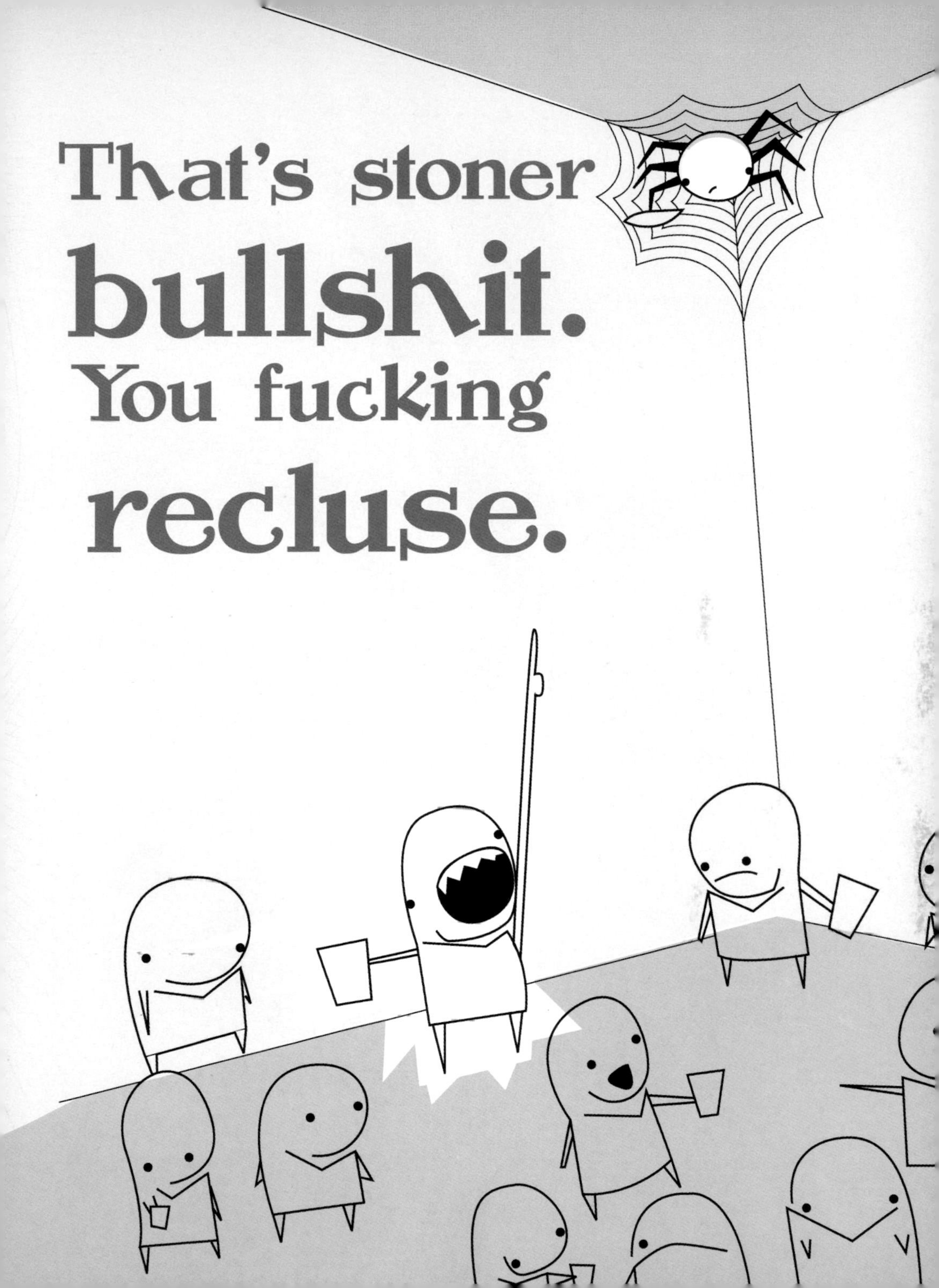
That's stoner
bullshit.
You fucking
recluse.

By now, you're either overcome with affection for or verbally assaulting everyone around you. When you were only Getting There, your inhibitions allowed you at least an iota of self-awareness. (i.e.: If you saw someone with an agreeable face, you panned right past. Now, there's a strong chance you're in each other's arms.)

...going... going ...

For the most part, you deem
it perfectly acceptable
to break social norms,
so you jump into someone
else's conversation, start
a fight or three, and lose
control of the volume of
your voice. You learn that
walking without actually
picking up your feet proves
sort of fruitless, and, if
you're that kind of drunk,
so is speaking without
spitting, leaning without
falling, and agreeing
without high-fiving.

The Going ... Going ...
stage is home to your
development of seemingly
intellectual stimulation.
It's where you talk about
your brooding childhood
("My father was never
really part of my life");
defend your (non)religion
("I don't believe in god,
but I believe in a 'higher
power'"); reveal sob
depression stories ("No
one really knows how sad
I am"); find that you are
being well-received; and
become yet another voice in
the very book you hold in
your hands.

DUDE
DON'T
TOUCH
THAT.

IT MIGHT HAVE

AIDS
ON IT.

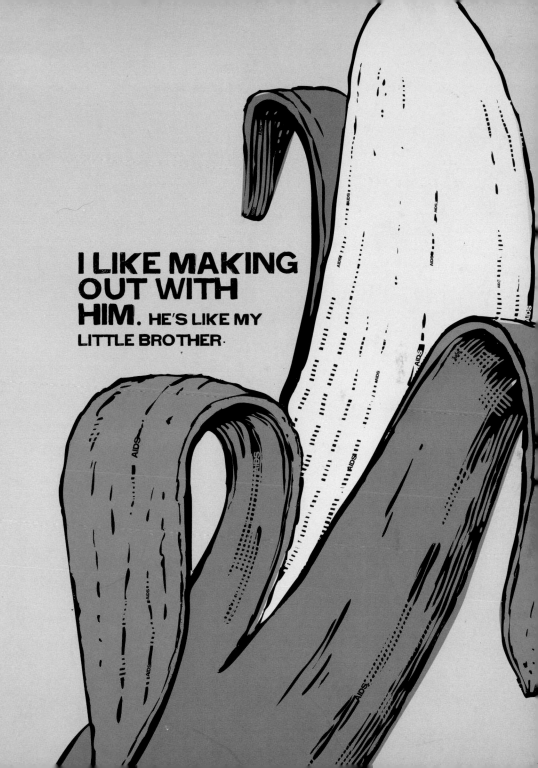

I'M NOT **SMOKING** WITH YOU.

Every time you smoke you get really horny
for 1 hour and then sleep for 5.

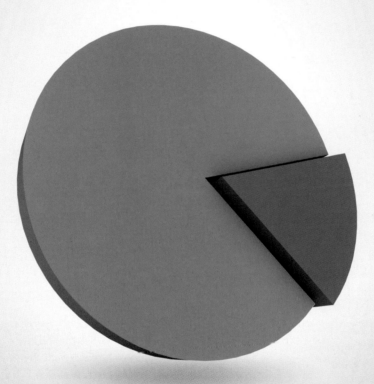

Time spent sleeping it off.

Time spent horny.

I DON'T GO CLUBBING LIKE I USED TO. LAST TIME I WENT TO THE CLUB I SAW LIKE THREE PREGNANT CHICKS DANCING LIKE THEY AIN'T HURTING NOBODY.

I meant to ask you, how was it having sex with my sister?

THERE'S SOMETHING
FLOATING IN YOUR DRINK.
DUDE, THAT'S JUST A LIME

NO , IT'S MOVING,
DUDE. IT'S MOVING!

AW, DUDE THAT'S NOT A LIME,

HEY, **DRINKS ON ME** TONIGHT. AND BY 'DRINKS,' I MEAN YOU...

... AND YOU.

YOU'RE ABOUT AS
EXCITING AS A
DUVET.

I'm only in town for one night,
and I haven't had sex
since November.

it's just a casual curiosity ...
like you, being bi.

I saw him at Wal-Mart buying Depends. I don't trust anything he says.

WRESTLING!

Turn your natural talent for groping men into meaningless trophies & medals!

I float like a stinger and fly like a bee!

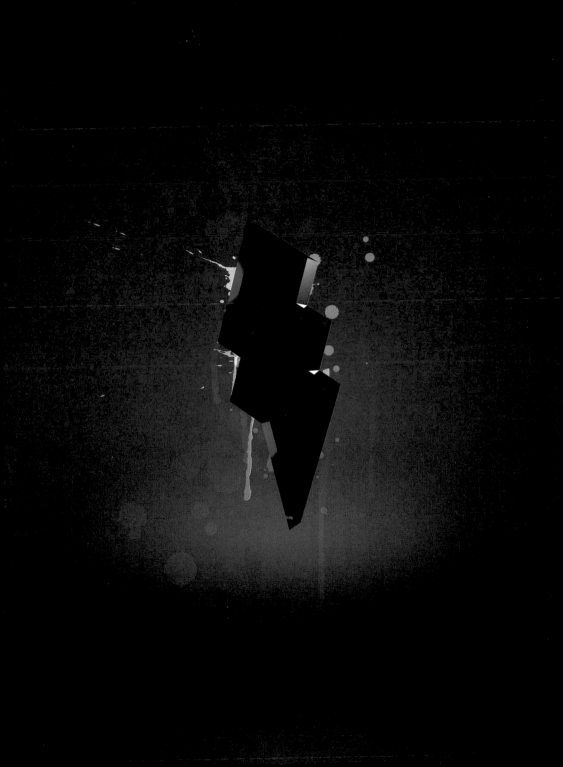

Twenty-two years' worth of decisions and this is where I end up.

If god wanted me to be drunk, I'd be drunk.

And I am.
I do what the man upstairs says.

ISN'T THAT THE STUDY OF SOMETHING?

'SODOMY' IS NOT THE STUDY OF SOMETHING.

look at her. do you
really think she'd want
to bone?

you gotta set limits for
yourself, man.

Oh, I
thought you
were on
ecstasy . . .
because of
the way
you were
dancing.

He made me hide in the shower while his ex-girlfriend got the rest of her stuff.

I mean, on one level, I can see where he's coming from.

Like, you can tell he didn't want to hurt her so he made me hide. I respect him for that. I do.

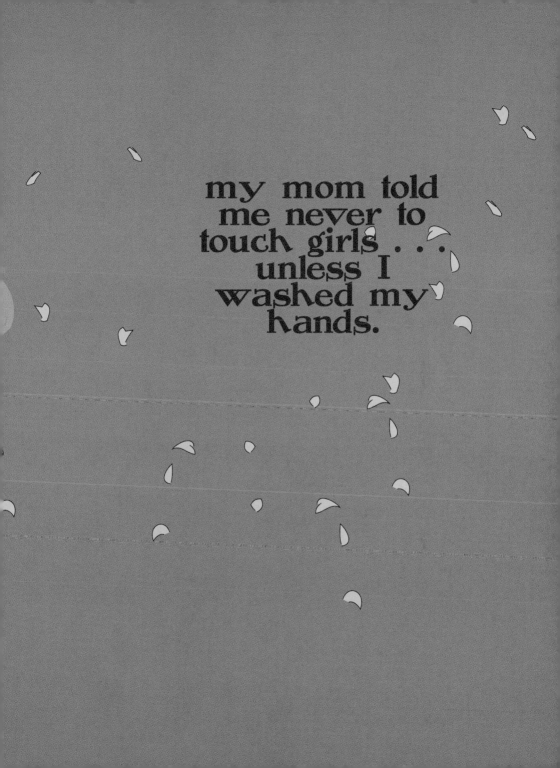

my mom told
me never to
touch girls . . .
unless I
washed my
hands.

The ride home is a bumpy
one. You can't decide
if closing your eyes is
better for your gurgling
stomach than leaving them
open. You're convinced
that hanging out of the
window helps. If you're
a conscientious sort of
intoxicated, you start
wondering if there's
anything in your purse
that will short-circuit
if you puke on it, and—
if you reach the point
of desperation—begin
visualizing starchy foods
like mashed potatoes and
french bread absorbing
the alcohol your liver has
rejected as poisonous. That
helps a little.

. . . gone.

The closer you get to
a toilet–or ground that
doesn't move–the more
you feel that first surge.
It's just so easy to keep
the first one down, but
not the second. Never the
second. The second surge
welcomes the realization
that the sole purpose of
your existence has been
dwindled to entertainment
for others.

Now's the best time to
accept the fact that at
this point, your speech
is nothing more than
a random selection of
coexisting sounds that your
acquaintances will throw
back to you over brunch.

If you've pissed out
or thrown up all your
willpower, you're probably
still out and about. This
means your lips must be
moving but no substantial
words that Merriam-Webster
would recognize are likely
being produced. Of course,
then there are these
people...

That shit smelled like it was **vacuum** sealed for years and I ripped it open and stuck my nose in it.

AS OPPOSED TO COLD CUM?

I make so many wrong
decisions. So many.
So so many.

SEE? THAT'S WHY I DON'T LET YOU IN MY BUTT.

I've only slept with like nine people, but three of them couldn't get it up so I don't really count those.

The only time I ever regretted having sex with her was after we had sex like thirteen times this one day and she kept blowing my cell up. I don't know, man.

Hope she's not pregnant.

it's as hot as a uterus in this bar.

what?

you think the clitoris
evolved from nothing?

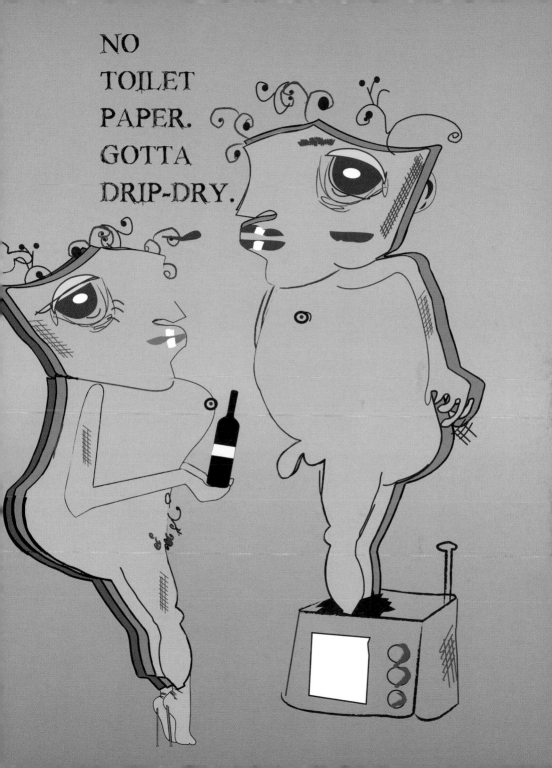

this
shot
has
the
faint
smell
of
public
restroom.

so just because i'm married,
i can't sleep around anymore?

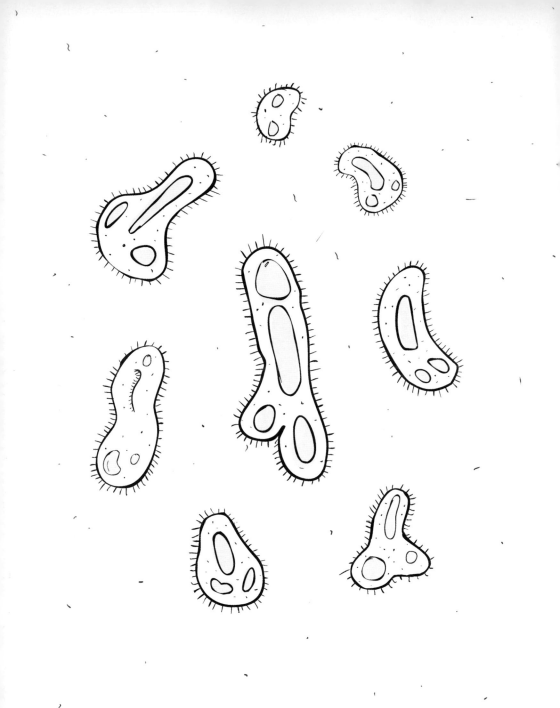

... BECAUSE WHEN HE GETS DRUNK, HIS PENIS IS MICRO-SCOPIC

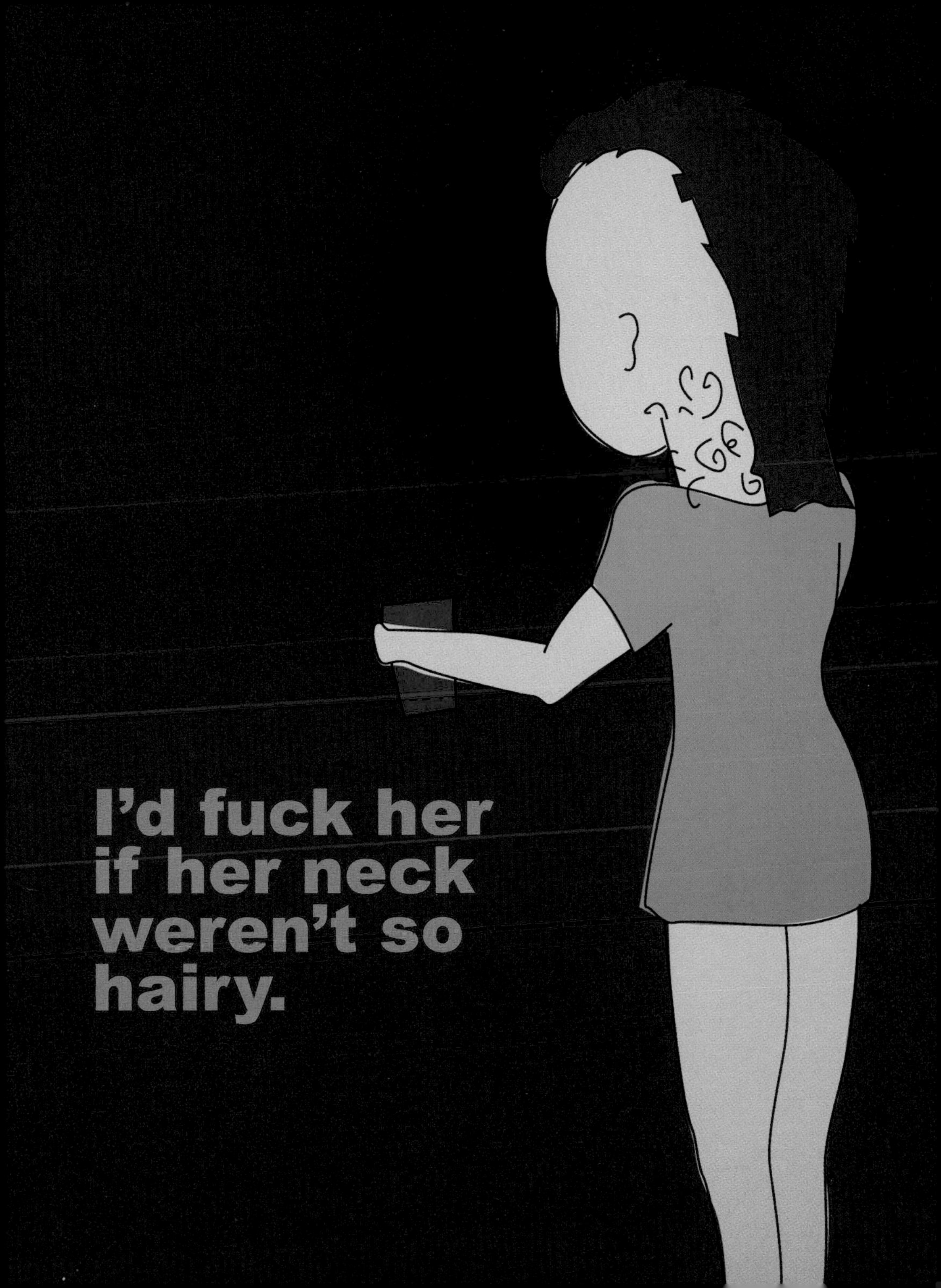
I'd fuck her if her neck weren't so hairy.

my lofty ambition
is to not throw up
on my in-laws at
brunch tomorrow.

I don't really care if you're hungry because I'm horny and nothing's coming out of that.

Seeing if she lets you do anal is like the ultimate test.

Yeah.
Yeah I'm
good. I...I
think I
just...I think
I just threw
up my soul.

it was beautiful. just cheap wine and candle light.

She smelled like passion fruit, lemon zest, and ky jelly.

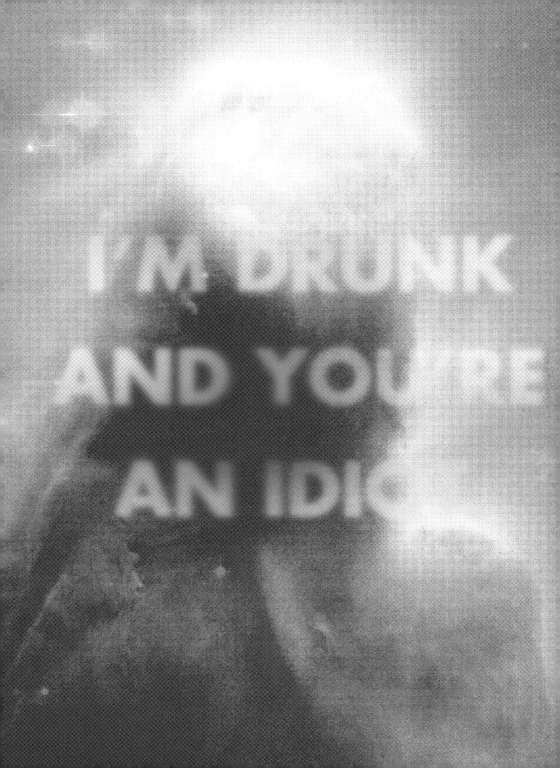

THIS HANGOVER KNOWS MY NAME.

MINIATURE HORSES ARE SO FREAKY

AND SHE FUCKIN GOES—SWEAR TO GOD MAN—SHE FUCKIN GOES,

"CUM ON MY FACE."

I ALMOST BLEW MY LOAD.

HE IS ONE SMOKING HOT TRANNY.

If a girl doesnt let you pee on her, it's like ok, where's this relationship really going?

MOVE, I'M ABOUT
TO POP A SQUAT.

I HAVE
ENTERED
THE BOWELS OF
DRUNKENESS

She pushed it away...
I call mine Franklin...and I'm still
climaxing, right? and THEN it manages
to shoot in MY eyes! I don't understand
how girls in pornos could pretend
to like that... THAT SHIT

BURNS!!!!!!!!!!!!!
oooooooooo

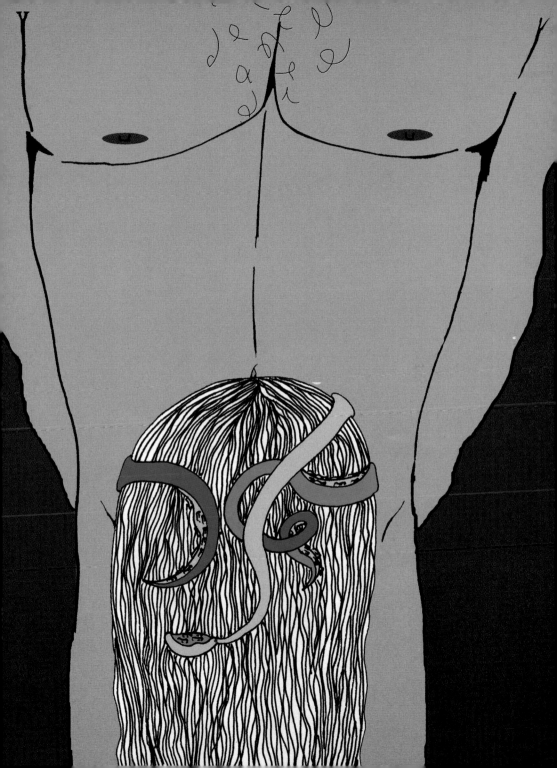

he's still standing there like we got more to talk about. whatcha want, boss? you wanna talk about it some more?

you wanna talk? you wanna talk about it? why you standin there?

why you standin there, boss? let's fuckin go, boss.

let's fuckin talk. come on! let's talk!

LET'S TALK!

"My favorite game is let's see who will step in my pee.

Everyone's a winner."

Don't girls feel non-secure or something when they period on you?

So anyway, I went to the bathroom and stuck my junk in bleach.

On a scale of 1 to drunk, I am trashed.

THEY MAY NOT HAVE BEEN LESBIANS BUT THEY DEFINITELY WANTED TO LICK MY VAGINA.

It's a strangely sad thing
to let these drunk quotes
die after one night.
When these quotes were
conceived, they generated
laughter, anger, smiles, and
wonder. They made moments
and ruined moments. And
for a moment, they seemed
to have meant everything...
but actually, little. The
idea behind this book was
to take something that was
ridiculous for a single
night, and turn it into
something timeless. Not
necessarily to relive the
moment, as it's clear that
many would have been better
left unlived in the first
place, but just for the hell
of it.

the morning
after

With the morning that
follows the night these
words were born comes a
strong chance you'll want
to take half the things
you said back. And if you
get stuck having slurred
at someone who isn't quick
to forgive, I hear the "I
was drunk" thing makes an
excellent fallback. So does
"I don't really remember
anything from last night."

But what about the things
you slurred that made it
to these pages? They're
embarrassing, revealing,
ruining. They might as
well have been written in
stone, because anyone can
hang them over your head,
now. That thing you've been
trying to forget has just
been leaked, clearly with no
regard to your reputation.
Exactly. Good times,
everyone. Keep talking.

Aaron Martin
superwindy.com

Adam Chang
sametomorrow.com

Bryant Castro
orangeglue.com

Joyce Krystal
papercannibals.com

Karen Kurycki
cmykaren.com

Katy Garrison
katygarrison.com

Philis Liu
philis.net

Sean Collins
monster8.net

Tim Allen
iamtim.me

Will Adams
extralush.com

the artists

I wouldn't have even wanted
to see this book come to
fruition had it not been
for the artists. You guys
carried this book into
production enthusiastically
and feverishly. Not many
people can take a bunch of
drunk quotes and turn them
into something visually
appetizing the way you all
did. Karen, Sean, Adam,
Smalls, Aaron, thank you.
Joyce, Katy, and especially
Bryant: a gigantic thanks
to you three. I wish your
names were on the cover
instead. Joyce, you are
what I hope to be someday.
Thank you for everything.
Abigail, your patience is
inspiring.

Skyhorse's Tony Lyons,
Ann Treistman, and Bill
Wolfsthal, sincere thanks
for taking a chance.

Will, your passion, talent,
and critical eye always
inspire me to give nothing
less than everything,
and create nothing less
than beautiful. This just
wouldn't have been as fun

without you. You mind-bottle
me.

To friends, friends of
friends, friends of friends
of friends, and complete
strangers who shared their
drunk quotes with me,
thanks a lot. There was
nothing quite like waking up
to your drunk texts, voice
messages, and e-mails. What
the hell. Keep 'em coming.

acknowledgments

your drunk quotes

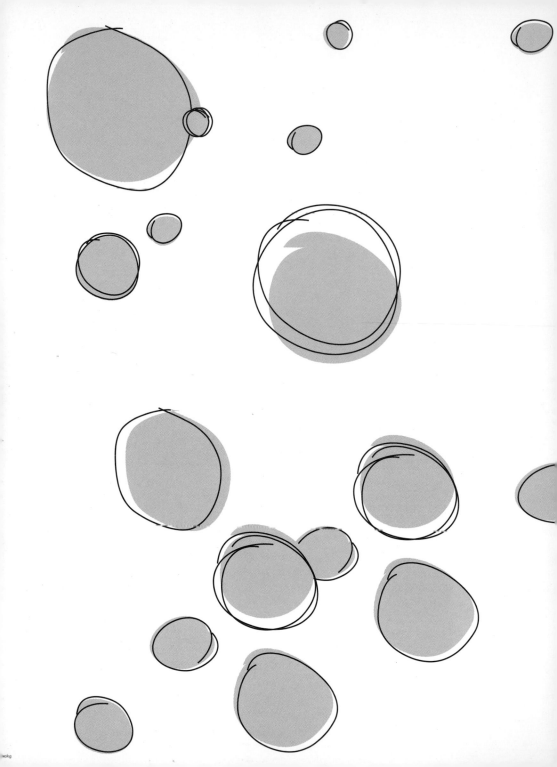